Modern Mandolin Method

The mandolin is used in nearly every type of music today so it is a great choice of instrument whether you like jazz, folk, classical, country, bluegrass, rock, blues, Irish or many kinds of world music. Much of this music is only available in standard notation so that is where we will start in this volume. By learning the basic information presented here, you will be prepared to approach any style.

If you are a first time string player, be sure to have a professional repair person look over your instrument making sure the frets, nut, neck, bridge and strings are in good shape. This is true of new and used instruments alike. Simple adjustments can make significant improvement in ease of playing. A well adjusted instrument will make learning a pleasure and is well worth the time and any expense. A reputable music store with a guitar repair department is a good place to find an experienced repair person.

Holding the Mandolin and the Pick

The mandolin can be held in the lap with or without a strap. Players who stand when they perform will obviously need a strap, but some players who always sit to play like the stability a strap provides. With or without a strap, the body of the mandolin should be centered on the players body with the neck angled up so the left hand can easily cradle the neck (fig. 1.) Make a "V" with your left hand thumb and first finger. The neck should be cradled in the top of the "V" between the first joint of the thumb and the bottom inside joint of the first finger where it joins the palm. The flat inside of the palm should not be in contact with the neck and there should be a "window" of space above the bottom of the "V" and below the neck (fig 2.) The neck should not be grasped like a baseball bat.

Unlike proper guitar technique, the left hand thumb may extend slightly above the mandolin fingerboard. In this position, the fingers should curve easily to fret the strings on the fingerboard. The thumb will generally be close to the first finger. When forming chords, the thumb may slip to the back of the neck to help get a clean sound on each note of the chord.

A flat pick (also called a *plectrum* in older method books) is held between the right hand thumb and first finger. Although each player finds their own comfortable position, begin by placing your right wrist behind the bridge top on top of the non ringing part of the strings (fig. 1.) The right hand thumb should be parallel to the strings with the pick pointed into the top of the mandolin on the "fleshy" pad under the thumbnail. The first finger holds the pick against the thumb (fig 3.) Try playing the low G strings with several downstrokes of the pick. Adjust the grip by adjusting the amount of "squeeze." Some players prefer to use the rounded shoulder of the pick rather than the point. You may find that, at first, the pick will move, turn or even fall out of your fingers. This is normal for beginning players and will happen less often with practice. Picks come in many thicknesses. A pick marked "medium" is a good place to start.

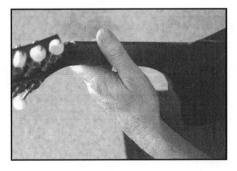

Figure 2

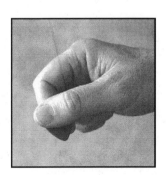

Figure 3

Figure 1

Tuning

To begin, you should be sure your instrument is in tune. Good string musicians take time, every time they play, to be sure their instruments are in good tune. Being out of tune is an unattractive sign of a beginner and it is an easy mistake to avoid. Strings are effected by temperature and humidity so even a well tuned instrument may require some adjustment as a practice session progresses. Many players enjoy the ease of using an electronic tuner. These devices use internal microphones or direct vibrations to "sense" the pitch of the four paired mandolin strings. By adjusting one of the eight tuning machines, you can change the pitch of the string until the needle is correct or a light comes on indicating that the string is in tune.

You can also tune by matching known "correct" piches from reliable sources such as electronic keyboards, well tuned pianos, guitars or on-line audio tuners. The four strings of the mandolin from lowest in pitch to highest are tuned G (below middle C,) D (above middle C,) A (above middle C) and E (one octave above middle C.) Although there are actually eight strings, mandolin players generally speak as if there were only four. Therefore, *the first string* refers to both first strings. We will do the same in this volume.

The Process

The lowest and "fattest" pair of strings is called the 4th or G string and it is the closest string to the ceiling as you hold the mandolin. Tune the first individual G string, closest to the ceiling, by turning the first tuning machine until the pitch is correct. Strike the string repeatedly whenever you are adjusting them. This way, you will hear if you have struck the wrong string or you are tuning the wrong direction. Failure to do this can result in broken strings.

If the string has been put on correctly, a counterclockwise turn will raise the pitch and clockwise will lower it. If the string is too low in pitch, turn the machine slowly until it reaches the correct pitch. If it is too high, lower the pitch of the string until it is below the correct pitch and then return to the correct pitch from below. Always tune from below the correct pitch. This will minimize slipping problems. Now tune the second G string to the same source until it is in tune. Finally, sound the two G strings together making sure they sound in tune together. If they do not sound in unison, as one, you may need to start over being careful to match the pitches accurately. Repeat the operation for each string until you reach the high E (1st) strings. Note that when you change sides of the peghead to tune the A and E strings, the directions change. Now a clockwise turn will raise the string and counterclockwise will lower it.

The entire tuning operation may take quite a while the first time, but it will get faster. It is time well spent. Mandolin music is written in the *treble clef* with much of the music occuring within the five lines of the musical staff. Learning to read standard music notation by sight for the mandolin is a simple process that can be learned easily by following the instructions and exercises given in this book.

Tuning methods in order of preference
1) Use an electronic tuner.
2) Match the tuning notes on the CD.
3) Match notes on a piano or keyboard.
4) Match notes on a well tuned string instrument.
5) Tune the mandolin to itself using the method below.

Tuning the mandolin to itself. Begin with a note that sounds "about right" for the G string.
1) Tune the Gs to each other, Now fret the G string at the 7th fret.
2) Adjust the D strings until they match the 7th fret G string D note.
3) Play the D strings at the 7th fret and match the A string to this note.
4) Repeat for the E string.
5) Take care to match notes exactly. Any mistake will be magnified as you change strings.

Types of Mandolins

The classic form of the mandolin is often called "bowl backed." Some old timers call them "tater bugs." This type of mandolin is often cheaply made and likely designed to be hung on a wall for looks. Italian and classical players often have expensive, well made versions of these instruments but they are rarely seen.

Flat or arch backed mandolins are much more common. Flat top and back instruments such as those made by Martin Guitars are well made, good playing instruments. Other reputable brands include Mid America, Weber, Flatiron, and some older Gibsons, especially the Army-Navy model. These instruments usually have a round sound hole on the top and are generally constructed like guitars.

The arched top, round hole mandolin is a popular model, These are generally designed after older pear shaped Gibson models known as the A model. These can be very good instruments depending on the brand and offer a lot of sound for the price.

Mandolins modeled after the Gibson F-5 are generally the most available mandolins today. This is likely due to their popularity in bluegrass music. These mandolins have the unusual F shape including a scroll on the body and peghead, f shaped sound holes and a carved top and back. Well made versions of these instruments cost many thousands of dollars. At the mid priced end of the market, better bargains are often available in an A model mandolin.

Asian import companies make most of the beginning mandolins on the market today. Brands include Fender, Michael Kelly, Morgan Monroe, Alverez, Ibanez, Eastman and others. Quality varies widely among these imports. so take an experienced mandolin or guitar player with you when you shop. American companies include Gibson, Breedlove, Weber, Collings, Ovation and many individual lutherers. Check sites like http://www.mandolincafe.com/ for a more complete listings and links to web sites.

Strings

Acoustic mandolin strings come in sets of 8. They have loops on one end unlike guitar strings that have metal balls on one end. Reputable brands include Martin, D'Angelico. LaBella, Martin, Gibson and many others.They are available in various metals (bronze and steel) and gauges ranging from light to heavy. Beginners will likely want light to medium strings. Keep an extra set of strings in the case at all times.

Changing strings on the mandolin for the first time can be a daunting task. Ideally, you should buy a set of strings and have a instrument repair person change them while you watch. If this isn't possible, here are a few tips:

1) Study both ends of the strings before you remove anything.

2) Remove the tail piece cover to reveal the end of the strings over the body. Not all mandolins have these shiny tail piece covers, but if you have one, remove it by sliding the cover towards the end of the body. These are held on by friction only and can be difficult to remove.

3) With the tail piece cover off, study how the strings are attached. There may be as many as 12 hooks on which to hook the loop end strings. Remember where the strings were hooked.

3) Look carefully at how the G strings are attached at the tuners. We will need to duplicate that attachment.

4) Loosen the 2 G strings *only* until they easily come off the hooks on the tail piece. Now the other end of the strings can be removed from the tuner posts by pulling them out of the holes and the used G strings can be rolled up and disposed of.

5) One at a time, replace the G strings. Be careful that the string is straight and is attached to the correct hook, slot in the bridge, slot in the nut and tuner post. Return the strings to the correct note.

6) Replace the other strings in pairs as above.

7) Stretch the strings and re-tune.

Picks

Picks are the least expensive accessory. They come in many materials and thicknesses, so try them all out. Beginners will likely want a thinner pick such as a Fender light or medium. Regular sized guitar picks are used on the mandolin. Do not buy small "mandolin" or "jazz" picks.

Lesson 1: First Note

Look at the 5 line staff below. The funny "S" shaped symbol at left of the staff is called a *treble clef* and is the only clef you will see in this book. Look at the first note and pick the open first string (closest to the floor.) Don't think "E," although it is an "E." The "naming" part of your brain is not involved in sight reading. Just see the note and play it. In the staff below there are 4 quarter notes per measure. Count to 4 repeatedly while picking the first string with a downstroke

Lesson 2: Our Second Note

Play the second string of the mandolin. It is an A note, but more importantly, notice it lies in the second space from the bottom of the staff. Play the exercise below counting to four in each measure.

Lesson 3: Notes 1 and 2

In the exercise below, the first two notes are mixed. Notice the position of each successive note without pausing to think of their names.

Lesson 4: Notes 1, 2 and 3

Here are the first 3 open strings beginning with D, the 3rd string. While measure 1 has quarter notes, measures 2, 3 and 4 have eighth notes counted one and two and three and four and. Two eighth notes equal one quarter note. They are picked with alternating DUDU pick strokes.

Lesson 5: All 4 Open Strings G D A E

Here are all 4 open strings including a new one - the 4th string G. Note these 4 notes fall on spaces. Beginning in measure 2, the notes are eighth notes. The length of two eighth notes equals one quarter note. They are counted *"one and two and three and four and."* Eighth notes are played with alternating pick strokes: down - up - down - up - down - up - down - up. Measures 1-3 have a filled out tablature staff below to help locate the indicated notes.

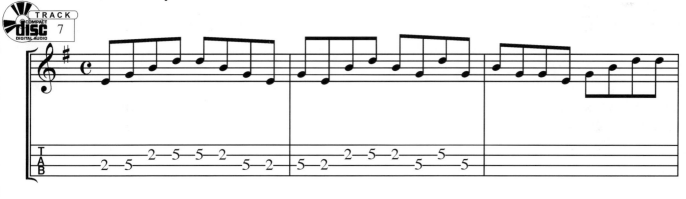

Lesson 6: E G B D

The 4 notes in this lesson are all on lines and they are all played at the 2nd and 5th frets. Also note that these notes are played with the first and third fingers. Play Lessons 5 and 6 until the 8 notes can be played without hesitation. Careful mastery of these two lessons is the basis for all that follows.

Lesson 7: Pick Direction

Pick direction is an important concern for developing flat pickers on guitars and mandolins. Well learned lessons here at the beginning will pay huge dividends as you advance as a player. The basic rules are simple but must be followed to achieve a professional sound. Down pickstrokes are indicated by a bracket over the note. The symbol "V" indicates an up stroke. Generally the movement should be through the string and not down toward the top of the mandolin or out away from the instrument. Strive for an even tone and volume from the down and up pick strokes. Practice down-up picking, changing strings as you play. If you "snag" in the strings. try to not play as deeply into the string with the pick. Several 32nds of an inch will likely be deep enough to strike the string.

Begin by playing downstrokes on the low G string (4) while you count out loud: *one, two, three, four*. Double the notes, adding up strokes after every down stroke, counting: *one and two and three and four and*. The example below puts in music the exercise described in the previous sentence.

If the note pattern changes, the rules stay the same. If you pat your foot as you play, you'll note the pick is down on the beat when the foot is down. Here are some variations using the D string (3).

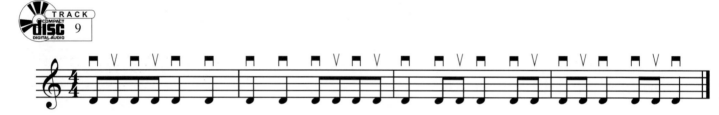

If rests occur on the downbeat, the first note may be an up stroke as in the measures below. This example uses the A string. Measure 1 below begins with an up because the first note occurs on the "and" after "one." In measure 2, the second up stroke (3rd note) occurs on the "and" after "two." If this is confusing look at this count for measure 2 (I use capital letters for "picked notes.") ONE AND two AND THREE AND FOUR AND. Down Up--Up Down Up Down Up.

Other exceptions may occur and they will be explained as they appear. This approach to pick direction is called *alternating picking* and is the basis for playing in many styles.

Lesson 8: Our First Tune

Here is an extended tune using eighth notes with the 8 notes we have learned. The melody is a somewhat simplified A part of the American fiddle tune *Leather Britches*. Listen to the CD for guidance. Use alternate pick strokes beginning with a down.

TRACK 11

Lesson 9: Lines

Hopefully you were successful with *Leather Britches* . If you had any problems, review the notes given up until now and strive to recognize and play them without hesitation. Now we'll learn the notes on all the lines.

The open tuning of the mandolin is in intervals of fifths as is its relative the violin. This has several surprising results for reading musicians. In this lesson, we learn that notes at the 2nd and 5th frets all fall on staff lines! The eight notes below are on lines and use the first and third fingers. The notes are all natural (not sharped or flatted) except the F♯ note at the second fret of the 1st string. These are the 4 notes you learned in lesson 6 plus 4 new ones.

I am indebted to violinist Christina Seaborn for pointing out this simple, but profound feature of violin tuning - that the notes on lines are played with the 1st and 3rd fingers,

TRACK 12

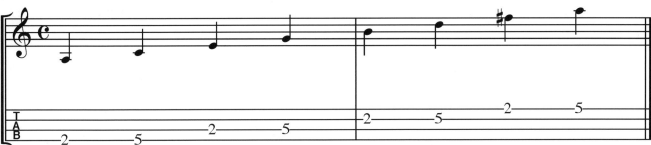

Lesson 10: Line Exercise

Here are six measures to practice for the line notes. Tablature will help get you started but you are on your own in measures 4-8. Listen to the CD.

Lesson 11: Spaces

The second part of Christina's surprise is that the spaces share a similar pattern. The notes in spaces are either open or played with the 2nd finger at the 3rd or 4th fret. In this example, the 3rd fret is used. The seventh fret note (B) in measure 3 is the highest note played in first position and the highest note that appear in this volume.

After you have played through this lesson, review all the previous lessons and make sure you are reading comfortably and without hesitation. Resist the temptation to "figure out" what a note is by playing from a known note. Also avoid using the mnemonic devices everyone was taught (FACE, EGBDF.) These methods will only slow down your reading and frustrate you. They are to be avoided.

Lesson 12: Space Exercise

The second finger is used to play notes at the 3rd and 4th frets in first position. On the 4th string these notes are Bb and B. On the third string they are F and F#. On the second string they are C and C#. On the 1st string they are G and G#. It is important to remember, regardless of the key, second finger plays the Bs (4th string,) Fs (3rd string,) Cs (2nd string) and Gs (1st string.) On the staff the notes look the same. The key signature determines whether the note is at the third or fourth fret.

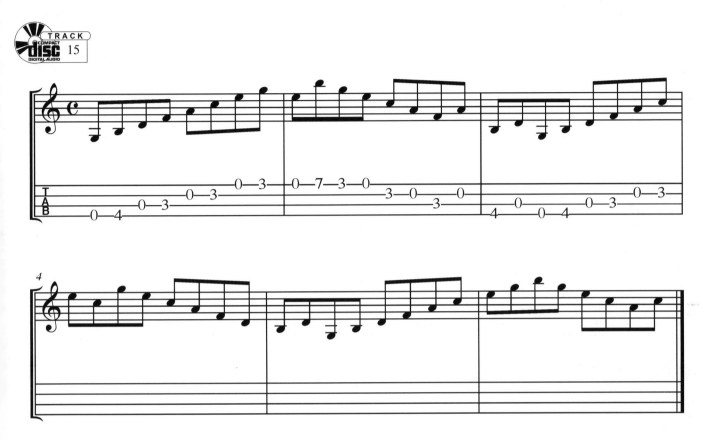

Lesson 13: Note and Rest Types

Notes and rests share the same names - whole, half, quarter and eighth. There are longer and shorter notes but these are the four discussed in this volume. In 4/4 time, a whole note gets 4 beats, a half note 2, a quarter note 1 and an eighth note 1/2 beat. Rests get the same time values. In each measure below, all 4 beats are accounted for. One whole, two halves. four quarters and eight eighths all add up to one full measure in 4/4 time.

Notice the whole rest"hangs" below the line while the half rest "sits" on top of the line. This simple story from grade school helps with memorization. *Two crows sat on a fence eating corn. The crow who ate until he was full fell under the wire while the half full crow remained upright.* A silly story to be sure, but you will never forget.

Lesson 14: The Key of G

The key of G has one sharp in the key signature. It is the F♯ on the top line of the staff. The convention wirh key signatures is that every note in all octaves in the signature is effected by the sharp or flat. This means on the mandolin in the key of G, the F at the third fret of the third string is also sharped (fourth fret.) Below is a two octave G scale in first position.

When beginning a new tune, a good habit is to first play the major scale of the key of the tune. This way your fingers are pre-placed for the correct sharps and flats in the music. The major scale below pre-places your fingers for Lesson 15.

Lesson 15: G Scale Practice

Here is a practice exercise using the notes of the G scale with half, quarter and eighth notes. Listen carefully to the CD track.

Lesson 16: Simple Gifts

This is a Shaker hymn used by Aaron Copeland as a theme in his orchestral work *Appalachian Spring*. It uses notes from the G scale with half, quarter and eighth notes. Review lessons 10 to 13 and listen carefully to the CD. The single note in the first measure is called a pickup note and the measure is the pickup measure. The pickup measure has only one beat and is often counted silently before playing begins. The pickup measure is not counted when numbering measures. The "C" symbol to the right of the key signature stands for the 4/4 time signature. "C" represents *common* time. Remember to pick down for quarter and half notes. Passages of eighth notes are played with alternating strokes beginning with down.

Lesson 17: A Common Fiddle Tune

It was once said of Texans, "They don't know the national anthem, but they all recognise *Turkey in the Straw!*" True or not, this melody at one time may have been the most well known of all American fiddle tunes. Here once again are some measures of G to practice before playing the tune.

Lesson 18: Turkey in the Straw

This tune is written in cut time (2/2.) It reads and picks just like 4/4 but is generally understood to be played faster. The rhythm in measure 10 is a new one and deserves some study. The quarter - eighth - quarter - eighth pattern counts like: *ONE AND two AND THREE and* where the capital words are new notes. This pattern is picked: DUUD. Listen carefully to the CD.

Lesson 19: Dotted Notes

A dot after a note adds one half the value of that note to its total duration. A half note lasts two beats in 4/4 time. A dotted half note lasts three beats (2+1.) A quarter note lasts one beat in 4/4 time. A dotted quarter lasts one and a half beats (1+1/2.) There are other possibilities, but these are to two kinds of dotted notes we will see in this volume. Rests are lengthened the same way.

Lesson 20: Finger Assignments and Note Names

Each left hand finger is responsible for 2 frets each. The 1st finger (index) plays frets 1 and 2. Finger 2 (middle) plays frets 3 and 4. Finger 3 (ring) plays frets 5 and sometimes 6. Finger 4 (pinkie) plays frets 7 and sometimes 6. Fingers 3 and 4 share responsibility for the sixth fret based on what note precedes the sixth fret. If, for example. the preceding note was a first fret note, the fourth finger would play the sixth fret note.

Each string of the mandolin has 4 unique note names in the 1st position.

	1st fret	2nd fret	3rd fret	4th fret	5th fret	6th fret	7th fret
G string :	G♯/A♭	A	A♯/B♭	B	C	C♯/D♭	D
D String:	D♯/E♭	E	F	F♯/G♭	G	G♯/A♭	A
A String:	A♯/B♭	B	C	C♯/D♭	D	D♯/E♭	E
E String:	F	F♯/G♭	G	G♯/A♭	A	A♯/B♭	B

Even though some notes have 2 names, string musicians tend to call them by only one. A, B♭, B, C, C♯, D, E, E♭, F, F♯, G and G♯ are the commonly used note names. The names A♯, A♭, G♭, and D♭ are seldom used in mandolin music. Generally, string musicians use sharps rather than flats with the exceptions B♭ and E♭.

Lesson 21: Scale Patterns

By now you may have begun to organize major scale patterns on the mandolin fingerboard. Here ts the entire 1st position scale in A. Solid black dots represent open strungs.

A major   A Pentatonic

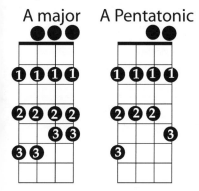

By memorizing the pattern, you automatically play the 3 sharps required in the key. Notice in the chord grid there are 2 helpful patterns. On the low strings the notes fall on the 2nd, 4th and 6th frets while on the high strings, the notes fall on the 2nd, 4th and 5th frets. A good habit to develop is to play the major scale in the key signature before beginning to read music in a given key. This way your fingers are prepared to play the correct notes for the key. Play the A major scale pattern several times from the lowest (on the left) to the highest. To the right on each major scale diagram is the major pentatonic (5 note) scale. These are very useful when improvising.

D major   D Pentatonic

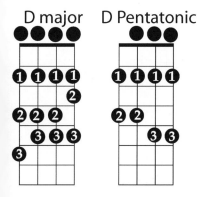

Strings 4, 3 and 2 of the D pattern look like strings 3, 2 and 1 of the A pattern. It is simply "moved over" one string. The first string is the only new pattern to memorize. Try playing this scale several times before reading *Soldier's Joy* and *Liberty*.

G major   G Pentatonic

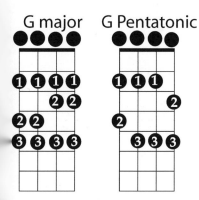

Another pattern helps memorization of the G scale. The low strings use frets 2, 4 and 5 while the high strings use frets 2, 3 and 5. Try this scale before playing *Turkey in the Straw*.

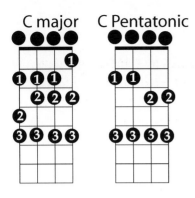

C major   C Pentatonic

The pattern in the key of C is less recognisable. The fret pattern on the 3rd and 2nd strings is 0, 2, 3, 5. All the notes are naturals as there are no sharps or flats in the key of C.

Lesson 22: The C Scale

Here in notation is the C scale shown in the diagram above beginning with the 4th string, 5th fret C note.

Lesson 23: C Scale Exercise

Here is a C scale exercise with a mixture of quarter and eighth notes. In order to hear the scale properly, begin on the fourth note (C) in measure 1.

Lesson 24: Texas Gals

Here is a 3 part tune in the key of C sometimes called "Texas Gales." Here in measures 5, 8 and 16 we have two notes over one another on the same staff. These are chords and are meant to be sounded together. They form common C chord shapes. Mandolin players sometimes borrow the violin teminology for these harmony notes and call them "doublestops." The double lines with two dots just to the right of the time signature on the first staff is a repeat sign. It indicates to play the music until you reach another similar symbol (the dots are placed before the lines in the second repeat sign.) Upon reaching the second symbol in measure 8, return to the first measure and repeat the 8 measure phrase for a total of 16 measures. Now note the repeat sign in meaure 9. Play 8 measures until measure 16 and then repeat 8 measures from measure 9, again for a total of 16 measures. Repeat at measue 17. If you wish to repeat the entire tune, play the first two staves twice followed by staves three and four twice and staves five and six twice.

There are several rhythmic challenges. Measure 1 counts: *ONE, TWO, THREE, AND four, AND*. The pick direction is DDDUU. Measure 12 plays: *ONE AND two AND THREE, FOUR.* (DUUDD)

Lesson 25: The Key of D

In many ways the key of D can be considered the home key of the mandolin. It falls in the middle of the instrument and the open D and A strings are the 1 and 5 notes of the D chord. Many favorite fiddle tunes are played on the mandolin in D. The key of D has two sharps. The first sharp is the F$\sharp$ we saw in the key of G. The second is the C$\sharp$. Play the scale indicated below and refer to the chart on page 15.

Lesson 26: D Scale Practice

Lesson 27: Liberty

The first 4 staves are a simplified version of an old American folk tune. Beginning on the 5th staff is primarily an eighth note version.

Version 2

Lesson 28: Ode to Joy

Here is a theme from Beethoven's Symphony Number Nine. In stays largely in the higher octave of D and therefore is a great exercise for notes above the staff. This arrangement also presents two and three note chords. Chords are indicated by multiple notes on the same musical staff line. The first note of the piece is a common D chord shape featuring the open 2nd and 3rd strings played with the 1st string fretted at the 2nd fret. This D chord is repeated in measures 4, 5, and 13. There are also dotted rhythms in measures 4, 8, and 16.

Lesson 29: Fainne Gael An Lae (The Dawning of the Day)

Irish poet Patrick Kavanaugh wrote words to this beautiful Irish air (melody) and titled the poem *Raglan Road*. This tune is in D and features dotted half, dotted quarter, quarter and eighth notes. It is good practice for all these note types and a good exercise for reading the lower octave of D. Listen to the CD.

Lesson 30: The Humours of Glendart - Duet Jig

The jig time signature is 6/8. The 6 means there are 6 beats per measure while the 8 indicates an eighth note get one beat. Repeat the name *Flanagan* to hear the rhythm. The eighth notes are grouped in two groups of three per measure and you should feel two pulses per measure. Up until now, the picking pattern has been to alternate eighth notes. On jigs, Irish musicians prefer to pick a measure of 6/8 as DUD DUD. (next page)

Two downstrokes played together in the middle of the pattern will seem odd at first, but this pattern better preserves the pulse of the jig. The harmony arrangement of this jig is unusual. Multiple players in Irish music typically play the melody together in unison. This is definitely a non-traditional arrangement.

Lesson 31: Chord Melody - Greensleeves

The practice of arranging melodies with chordal accompaniment is a popular approach on the guitar. While the full range of the guitar is not available, the mandolin can effectively play the style and shine as a solo instrument. If you experiment with this, try to voice the melody note on the highest string played in the chord. This is usually the 1st or 2nd string. Several re-occuring three note shapes appear in this approach. This tune is in 3/4, so remember dotted half notes get three beats. Tablature is included here to help you play the proper forms. Throughout this piece, notes "outside" the key signature are notated with sharps and flats (measures 6-7,) This will be explained later.

Lesson 32: Chord Melody II: What a Friend

Here is another familiar melody arranged in the chord melody style. The simple melody allows for many inventive re-harmonizations. Again sharps and naturals (accidentals) appear throughout and these will be discussed later.

TRACK 33

Lesson 33: The Key of A

The key of A has 3 sharps - F♯, C♯ and G♯. The F♯ and C♯ appear in the D key signature so G♯ is the new note. Once again, if you memorize the A scale pattern below, you will automatically play the correct notes for the key.

Notice the two patterns made here by the scale. On the G and D strings it is 2,4,6, 0 and on the A and E strings it is 0, 2, 4, 5. These patterns are a result of the fifths tuning of the open strings and it makes memorization of new scales quite easy.

The exercise below will check your familiarity with these new notes. If you are at all hesitant, review this lesson and listen to the CD for help.

Lesson 34: A Reading Exercise

Lesson 35: Devil's Dream

Here is a classic American fiddle tune that appears in a slightly altered form in Celtic tradition as *The Devil Amoung the Tailors*. The move in measure 3 from the 2nd note (F♯) to the 3rd (B) requires a finger roll from the 1st to the 2nd string or a hop of the finger from one string to the other.

Lesson 36: Ties and Slurs

Ties are arcs that connect two notes of the same pitch. The two half notes an measure 1 below are conected by a tie. The first note is picked and then is allowed to sound for the combined duration of the two notes.

The arc in measure 2 below connects two notes of different pitch and is called a *slur*. The H above the slur indicares a *hammer-on*. This left hand ornament involves striking the string and then forcefully fretting the string with a quick motion causing the string to continue sounding at the new pitch.

The slur in measure 3 is a *pull-off*. This left hand ornament involves striking the fretted string and then forcefully plucking the string with a quick motion causing the string to continue sounding at the new pitch.

The slurs in measures 4 and 5 are *slides*. The first note is picked and then after the duration of the first note, the finger slides to a new fret allowing the string to continue sounding.

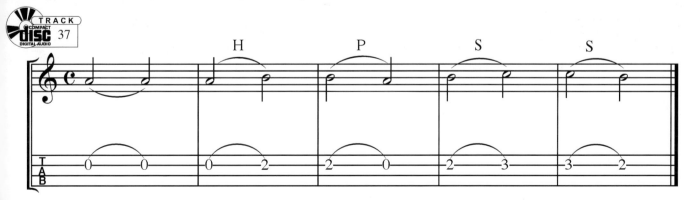

Lesson 37: Wilson's Wilde

Originally written for the lute, this anonymous renaissance tune is a favorite among classical guitar players. It is thought to have been written around 1590. This mandolin arrangement was written by multi-instrumentalist Gerald Jones and is used by permission. The piece is written in 3/4.

Lesson 38: Chords

Chords are important to any mandolin player who wishes to provide accompaniment to a voice or other instrument. A chord is usually defined as a combination of three or more pitches sounded simultaneously. While many mandolin books show chords involving all four strings, the author prefers 3 note chords for many musical situations, especially chords formed on the lower 3 strings.

The reason for this involves the relative high tuning of the mandolin. Guitar players may be aware the first string E of the mandolin is the 12th fret of the guitar first string. This means any note played on the mandolin E string is in the octave above the 12th fret of the guitar. Chordal instruments such as pianos and guitars play rhythm in middle and lower octaves. To better blend in with other rhythm instruments, the author prefers to play chords on the lower 3 strings of the mandolin. Some musics, however, such as bluegrass and some new acoustic music, do feature the higher chord sounds of the mandolin.

Chords come in many varieties, but most of them can be classified as a member of one of just a few chord families. We will concentrate here on three families: major, minor and dominant.

Major is the most common of chord types. Major chords are made from the 1st, 3rd and 5th notes of the particular major scale we are working with. This is called the chord formula. For example, a C scale consists of the notes: C, D, E, F, G, A and B. The 1st, 3rd and 5th notes are C, E and G. Any combination of these notes (in any order low to high) is a C major chord. These chords can be extended to become: 6th, major 7th, major 9th and others but they will still have 1, 3 and 5 in their formulas.

The formula for **minor** chords is the 1st, flatted 3rd and 5th notes of the scale. In C, this is C, E♭ and G. To flat a note, lower ts pitch one half step or one fret. These minor chords can be extended like the major chords to minor 6th, minor 7th, minor 9th and others. Despite any added notes, they wlll always have 1, ♭3 and 5.

The third family we will discuss is the **dominant** family. The most familiar chord in this family is commonly called the seventh chord and is written with the letter and the number seven (ex. C7.) There may be some confusion about this chord since its formula is the 1st, 3rd, 5th and flatted 7th notes of the scale. *The note that makes the 7th chord is a flatted 7th note not the 7th note.* Why? That discussion is for a music theory book. Just know the formula for a 7th chord is 1, 3 , 5 and flatted 7. The chord made by 1, 3, 5 and 7 is called a major seven and is a major, not a dominant, chord. The dominant family is quite large and includes 9th, 11th and 13th chords and various alterations to additional notes such as sharp and flat 5s, 9s and more.

The great thing about chords is that you don't need to know the scales and formulas to figure out how to form them. You can easily memorize your favorie major, minor and dominant shapes. With only two or three memorized shapes of each chord form, you'll be able to play nearly any song,

A SPECIAL NOTE ABOUT MANDOLIN CHORDS:

Many chords have more notes than the four strings of the mandolin. A Gm9♭5 chord for instance consists of 1, ♭3, ♭5, ♭7 and 9 (5 notes.) The mandolin player can not play all five notes and perhaps the remaining four will be impossible to play. For these extended chords. we have to decide which notes are "expendable" and which notes are likely to be played by other musicians in the group. The one note (root or tonic) is often provided by the bass, piano or guitar so it is "lose-able." The flat 3rd establishes this a minor chord. so we probably want to keep it. The 5 could normally be eliminated, but since it is a flat 5, we had better keep it. The flat 7th also helps define the nature of the chord so we'll keep it. The 9th is a color note and although it would nice to have, our Gm7♭5 chord will sound nice with the Gm9♭5 in the chart. These are the kinds of decisions required when you play large chords on the mandolin. Luckily, you will not usually have to make these decisions. You will simply memorize your favorite fingerings of the chord types you commonly encounter

Lesson 39: Basic Chords

Here are some basic open chord major, minor and 7th forms arranged in the circle of fifths. The diamond shaped dots represent the root notes (names) of the chord.

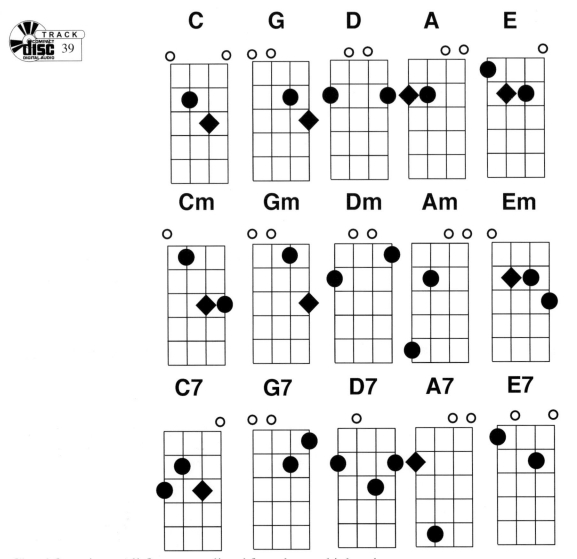

Chord fingering - All fingers are listed from low to high strings.

The C and G chords are fretted the same way using the 1st and 2nd fingers. The D also uses the 1st and 2nd. The A can be played with fingers 2 and 3 with very close placement. The E uses fingers 1, 2 and 3 - very close. The 3rd fret notes in the C minor chord can be barred by laying down the 2nd or 3rd finger. The G minor is fingered like the G major. Dm uses fingers 2 and 1. Am minor uses fingers 3 and 1. A 1st finger barre can be used in E minor. Fingers 2, 1 and 3 form C7. Fingers 2 and 1 form G7. Fingers 2, 3 and 1 form D7. Fingers 1 and 3 form A7 and fingers 1 and 2 form E7.

Lesson 40: Chord Exercise

Use this exercise to practice both the basic and movable chord forms on the next page.

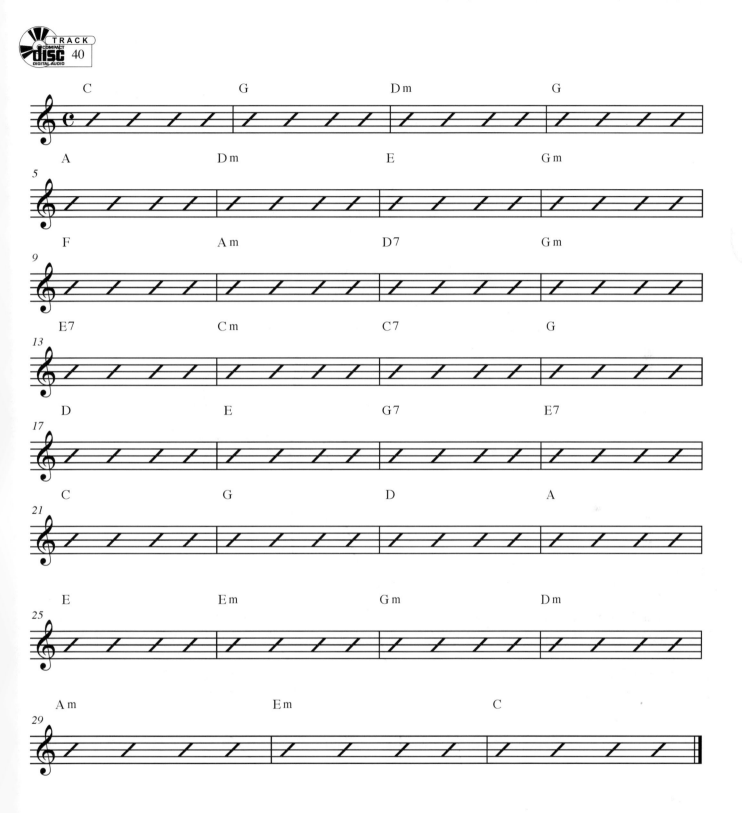

Lesson 41: Movable Chords

These forms have no open strings and therefore can be moved up or down the neck. The French word *barre* means to fret more than one string (at the same fret) by laying the finger flat on the fingerboard.

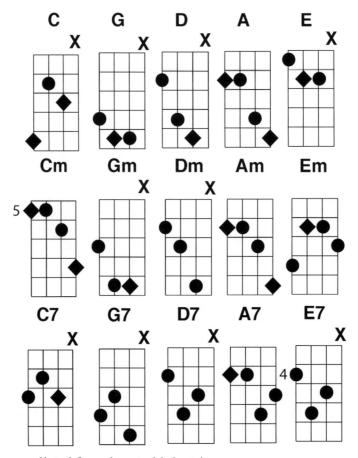

Chord fingering - All fingers are listed from low to high strings.

The C chord is fretted with fingers 3, 1 and 2. Strive to mute or kill the vibration of the 1st string. The G chord uses a 2nd finger barre and the 1st string is again muted. The D uses fingers 1, 3 and 4. The A uses a 1st finger barre at the 2nd fret and fingers 3 and 4. The E is fingered like the G. The "5" next to the C minor diagram indicate that the 1st finger barres at the fifth fret. Fingers 2 and 4 finish the chord. The G minor is fingered with the 1st finger and a 3rd finger barre. Dm uses fingers 1, 2 and 4. Am minor uses a 1st finger barre and fingers 2 and 4. A 1st finger barre can be used in E minor. Fingers 2, 1 and 3 form C7. Fingers 2, 1 and 3 form G7. Fingers 1, 3 and 2 form D7. A 1st finger barre and fingers 2 and 4 form A7 and fingers 1, 3 and 2 form E7.

Lesson 42: 3 Movable/Changeable Chord Forms

The A, G and D forms on the left of this page generate all the other chords here. The A form chord numbers spell 1, 5, 3, 1 from low to high. The first 4 chords on that line move the 1st string only to get Major 7 (1 5 3 7,) 7 (1 5 3 7) and 6 (1 5 3 6.) The A minor chord lowers the 2nd string (1 5 ♭3 1.) The other chords are produced by lowering the 1st string one fret at a time. Seven chords generated by one form!

The G form can be altered the same way. The chord numbers here spell 3, 5, 1 from low to high. We can make the same seven chords by altering notes as before.

Form three (D) spells 5, 3 , 1. The same changes produce seven new chords. From 3 forms we have made 21 chords.

From left to right, these chords are called Major, Major Seven, Seven, Six, Minor, Minor Major Seven, Minor Seven and Minor Six.

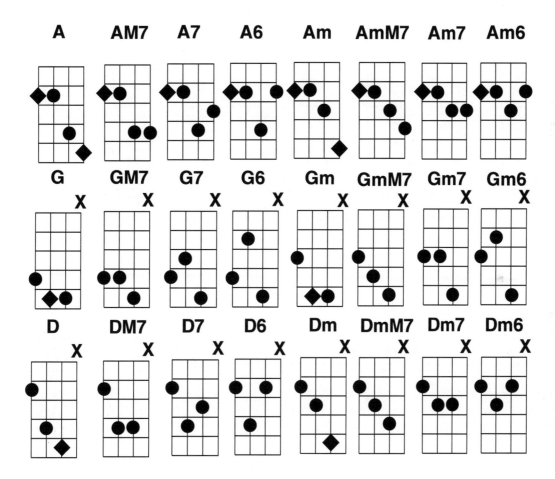

Lesson 43: The House of the Rising Sun

Here is a tune in 12/8 time that features arpeggiated chords throughout. In 12/8 there are 12 eighth notes per measure and each one gets a beat. They are grouped in 4 groups of 3. All the notes come from familiar basic chords shown in the previous diagrams. The accidentals that appear in measures 2, 4, 6 and 7 are sharped notes that don't appear in the key of C. The natural sign (♮) that appears late in measure 2 indicates a return to F from F♯. The accepted rule is that an accidental is "in force" for one measure unless it is cancelled by a natural as it is here. We will learn more about accidentals later.

Lesson 44: The Harmonized Scale in Sixths

This lesson may be one of the most important in this volume. Many players have successful careers on the mandolin knowing only the information on this page. Play the eight two note shapes shown in the first line. This is the G major scale harmonized in sixths. Many players use their 1st and 2nd fingers for the "close" (1 fret) shape and fingers 1 and 3 for the 3 fret (apart) shape. It may help memorization to think of the order of shapes as: together, apart, apart, together, together, apart, apart, together.

The second line of chords represents the C harmonized scale. Note the name of the higher note in the beginning shape names the scale you are playing, i.e. the third fret of the E string is G (line 1), the third fret of the A string is C (line 2.)

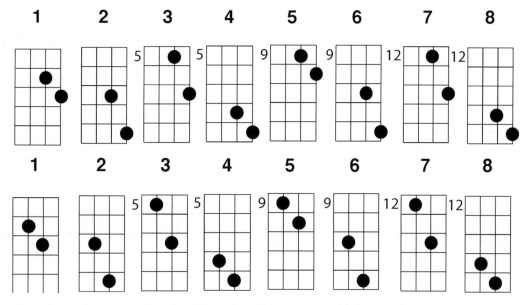

Experiment using these shapes to play familiar melodies. For instance, the standard *Sentimental Journey* can be played with this sequence of shapes: 31 31 31 31 31 31 34 33 2. *Brown Eyed Girl* and *Margaritaville* are also easily found in these shapes.

Once you are familiar with the pattern, try moving the pattern up a whole step to A or D. Ultimately, realize that every key is available as long as you can place the beginning shape at the correct frets and play the pattern. Many mandolin players use these shapes to accompany guitar playing singer/songwriters. Even without rehearsal, knowing the key and playing the pattern will often provide satisfying results.

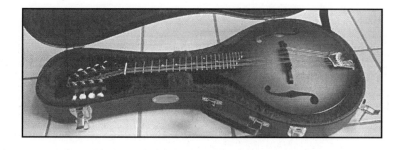

Photo by Gerald Jones. Used by permission.

Lesson 45: Accidentals

Accidentals are symbols that over-ride the key signature and effect notes by half steps. They include sharps (♯,) flats (♭) and naturals (♮.) Accidentals are "in effect" for only the measure in which they appear. After that measure, the notes return to those indicated in the key signature. The example below is in the key of D. The key signature indicates that all the F and C notes in the piece should be sharped (raised one fret or half step.) In measure 1, however, a natural symbol before the first F note makes this F note, and any F notes that follow in this measure, natural. In measure 2, the Fs return to the sharped variety as they are now controlled by the key signature.

To be very clear, the 5th note in measure 1 is F natural because of the natural accidental. The 7th note in the measure is also F natural because the natural symbol is still in effect. In measure 2, the 1st note is an F sharp because the natural symbol is no longer in effect and the key signature indicates F♯. In some situations like this the writer of the music may provide a *courtesy accidental* to remind the player that the natural symbol is no longer in effect. Other writers may just assume the player knows the rule.

TRACK
COMPACT
disc 45

Be aware that some notes have two names, C♯ and D♭, may appear in different scores but they are the same note on the mandolin. The next example shows both notes. Because C is a second finger note and D is a third finger note, string music writers often use note names to indicate which finger should be used.

In the example below, the second finger plays the C and C♯ notes in measure 1 as it would the C♯ and C notes in measure 2. In measure 3, the second finger plays C, C♯ while in measure 4, the third finger plays D♭ and the second finger plays C.

TRACK
COMPACT
disc 46

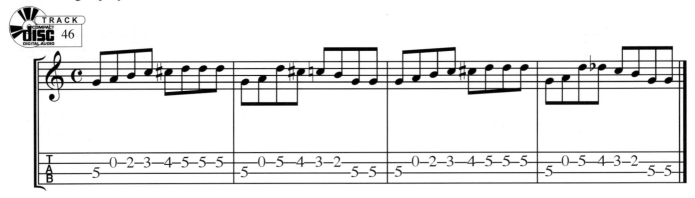

Lesson 46: Tremolo

To the casual listener of mandolin music, the rapid repeating notes of the classical or Italian mandolin player is **the** mandolin sound. The technique is used to give the illusion of sustained notes that otherwise would decay very quickly. Tremolo is produced by rapid down up down up movement of the pick. The exact speed of the tremolo varies from player to player and from style to style. It can be said generally that classical and Italian music uses a faster tremolo while folk and country styles are slower.

Players who use this technique often may find that a somewhat thinner pick is easier to use. Players who use a thicker pick may find loosening the grip on the pick makes the technique easier. The pick should "re-angle" between the thumb and first finger of the right hand as you play down-up strokes. It the pick gets "hung up" in the strings, try playing more shallowly – meaning to not put to pick deep into the string, but play lightly across the top of the string. Some players find using the soft curved shoulder of the pick rather than the point helps develop a smoother tremolo. Others plant their 3rd and 4th fingers on the mandolin top during tremolo passages.

To develop tremolo, begin by playing exercise 1 below. The measures 1 and 2 are based on four groups of 16th notes. The first note each group (a downbeat) should get a downstroke accent. Measure 3 and 4 show the standard way of indicating tremolo by placing two sideways hash marks across the note stems.

The tremolo in measure 3 has two hash marks across each note and is called *measured tremolo*. This means there are specific numbers of notes per beat, usually four, six or eight. When notes appear with two hash marks as in measure three, they are to be played as in measures 1 and 2. Practice with a metronome striving for an even sound without accent at first. Only after you have developed a steady tempo, even volume tremolo, add the accents to the first of each group.

Below, we have a two octave G major scale marked for measured tremolo. Remember, four sixteenth notes per quarter note. Strive for a even sustained sound as you play up and down the scale,

Lesson 47: Romance

This well known classical guitar piece is played by guitarists of all levels. On guitar, the melody is played with the 1st and 2nd fingers as notated here on the first string while the thumb plays accompanying bass notes. As a developing tremolo style mandolin player, we can use this melody as an exercise to help develop a strong measured tremolo with no stutters or missed notes. Accent the first downstroke of each new note to help define the melody.

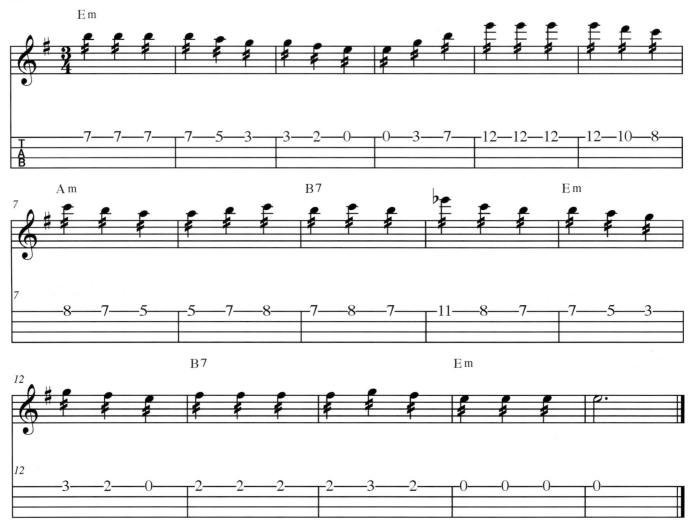

Three hash marks across a note indicates *unmeasured tremolo*. There are no specific numbers of strokes per beat in unmeasured tremolo although six or more is common. The sound difference between these two tremolo types is subtle and requires many hours of practice to master. While tremolo is only an occasionally played element for general mandolinists, it is an important required skill for classical and Italian style players. If you want to master this demanding technique, commit to many hours of focused, metronome-assisted practice.

Lesson 48: Santa Lucia

Here is a popular Italian melody marked for unmeasured tremolo. Stay relaxed and strive for an even sound.

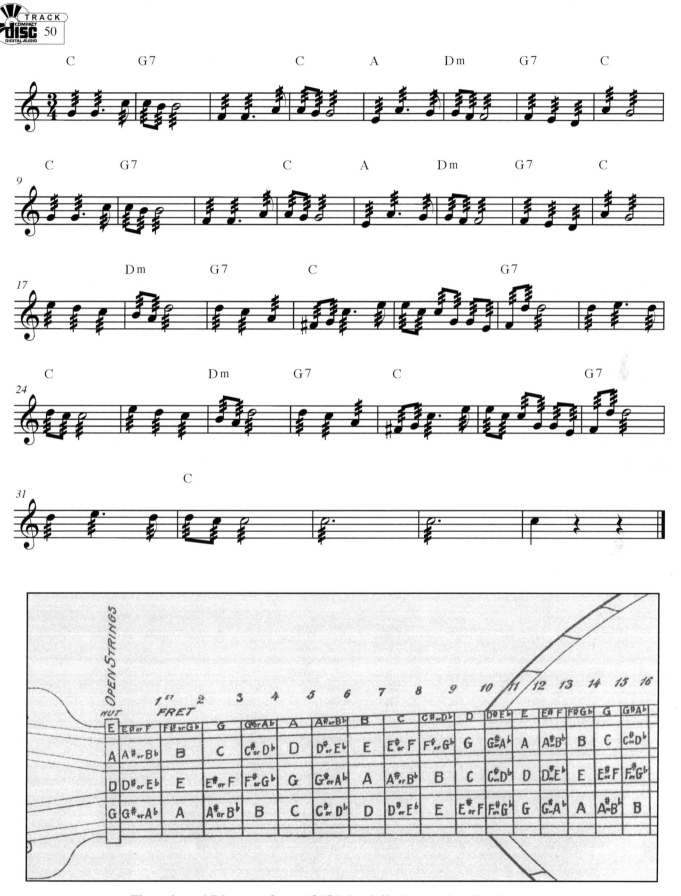

Fingerboard Diagram from 1898 Mandolin Instruction Book

Lesson 49: Leyenda

Here is a popular classical guitar piece re-arranged for the mandolin. The guitar arrangement is in E minor and uses the repeated second string, a B note on guitar. On the mandolin, the A string is used and the resulting arrangement is in D minor. This piece is great down-up alternating pick practice especially beginning in measure 16 as the two strings involved become the 2nd and 4th strings.

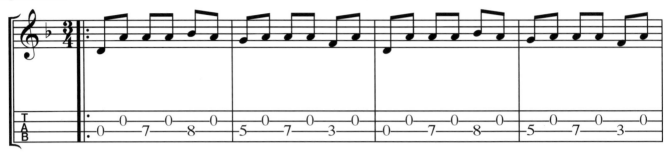

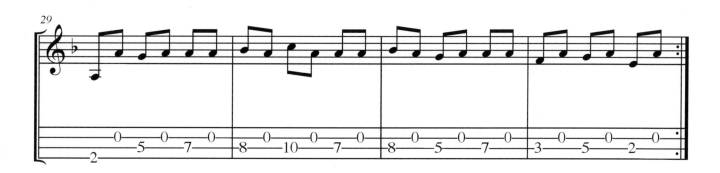

Lesson 50: Las Mañanitas

Here is a traditional Mexican birthday song in the key of G. The first four measures are an introduction. This song is good practice for the dotted quarter note and eighth note combination. The small note in measure 17 is called a grace note. See that it is attached by a slur to the larger D note. This indicates a very quick slide with the third finger from the 4th fret to the 5th.

Lesson 51: Bach Minuet

This minuet in the key of G features accidental C sharps in measures 20 , 21, and 23. The small arc in measure 9 connecting the two A notes is called a *tie*. Play the eighth note A only and allow it to sound for the combined time of the two notes - 2 1/2 beats.

Lesson 52: Lesson for Two Lutes

This is an anonymous duet that is popular among classical guitar players. The first CD track features the duet played by two mandolins. This mandolin arrangement was written by multi-instrumentalist Gerald Jones and is used by permission.

Lesson 53 Harmony in Thirds - C

Just as sixths are, thirds are useful intervals for soloing and backup. The patterns are less recognisable than sixths, but the extra effort is well worth the time. The major scales, in the nine keys covered in this book, are presented on an available space basis in the remaining pages of this book. The committed student will memorise these lessons. The examples present the intervals in two octaves for completeness. Play only as high as you can practically reach. Thirds above the 12th fret will likely too difficult to finger.

Lesson 54 Key of E

So far, we have concentrated on sharp keys in this volume. This is the case because generally, strings like sharps and horns like flats. We have studied the keys of C (no sharps or flats,) G (1 sharp,) D (2 sharps) and A (3 sharps.) The key of E has 4 sharps. It is even more important here to memorize the scale shape to insure the proper notes for the key. You may notice the E scale fingering is like the key of A "moved over" one string. In measures 1-3 below is the E major scale. Start on the E note (sixth note in measure 1) to hear the sound of E. The first five notes are in what I call "half position" meaning the first finger is in the 1st fret. Use the 1st finger for both the 5th (1st fret) and 6th (2nd fret) notes in order to return to standard 1st position.

In measure 4 is the E major arpeggio just using the 1, 3 and 5 notes of the E major scale. Measure 5 and 6 feature the E major pentatonic scale This five note scale removes the 4 and 7 notes. Since these are notes that can sound "wrong" if used at the wrong time, the major pentatonic is a great "safe" improvising scale.

In measures 7 and 8 are all the possible E "double stops" in first position. These 2 note shapes are great tools for making up solos or backup.

Play through these 8 measures before moving to the E reading song.

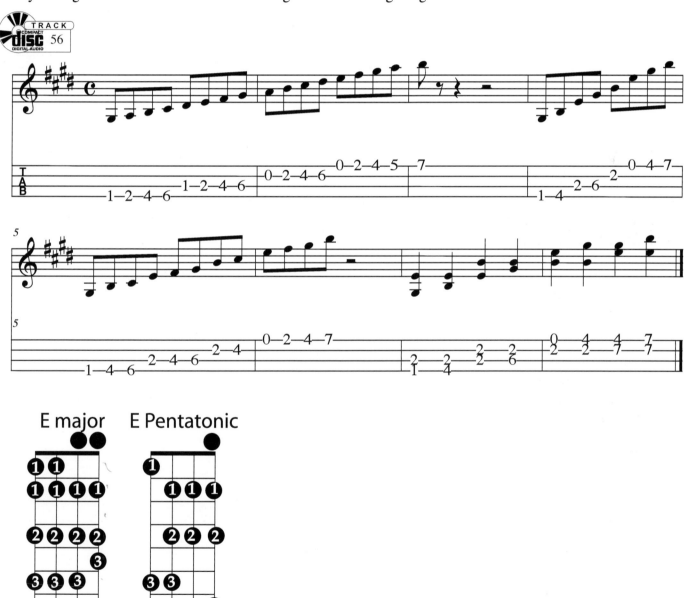

E major   E Pentatonic

Lesson 55: Hard Times

This beautiful Stephen Foster song makes a great reading exercise in the key of E. The first 3 staves are all played at frets 2, 4 and 6 of the D and A strings.

Stephen Foster

Lesson 56: Key of F

The key of F is our first flat key. It has a B flat note and spells F, G, A, B♭, C, D, E and F. Many experienced mandolin players consider F a "hard key" without actually trying it out. Play through the exercise below. Other than the 1st frets for the 2nd string, B♭ note and the 1st string F note, it is a very normal playing scale.

As with the E scale, the major scale is presented first. Begin by playing on the F note (6th note) to hear the proper major sound. Next in measure 4 is the major chord arpeggio followed by the major pentatonis scale. Finally, there are the first position double stops.

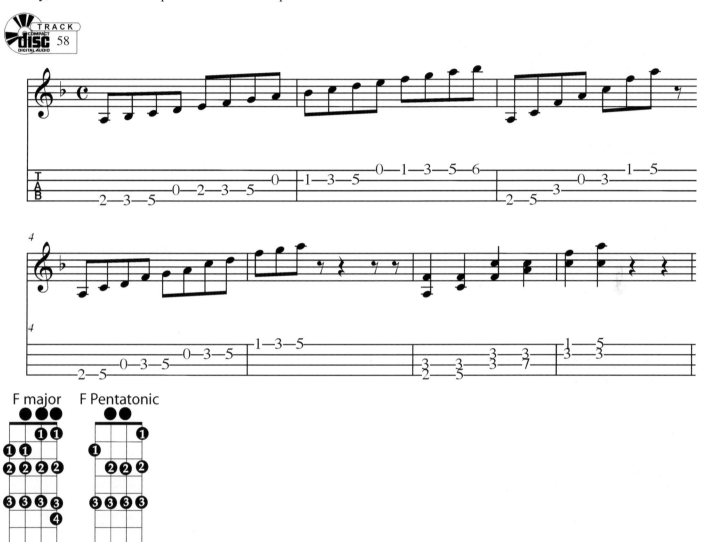

Lesson 57 Harmony in Thirds - F

The first three notes are presented alone. The thirds begin on the third eighth notes in measure 1. The entire exercise as presented is easily reachable as less than 2 octaves are shown.

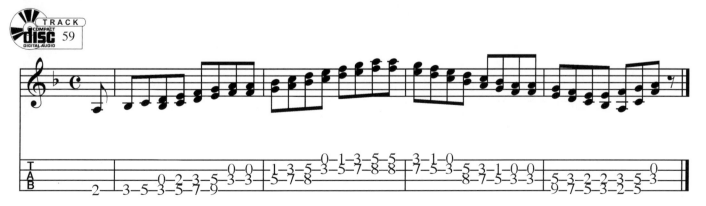

Lesson 58: Nearer My God to Thee

This hymn is famous for reportably being the tune the Titanic string orchestra played just before the liner sank. It is interesting to note that although this hymn is in F, there are no B♭ notes here! It really feels like playing in the key of C. Notice staves 2 and 4 are identical. It can be played with all downstrokes.

Lesson 59: The Key of B♭

TRACK disc 61

B♭ has 2 flats - B♭ and E♭. Below is the major scale followed by the arpeggio, major pentatonic scale and the first position double stops. Memorize the scale pattern before reading *Amazing Grace*.

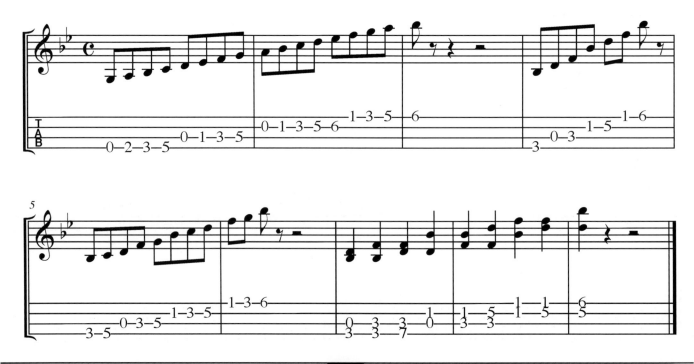

Lesson 60: Amazing Grace

This hymn is so universally known that it almost plays itself. Proper hand position makes it even easier.

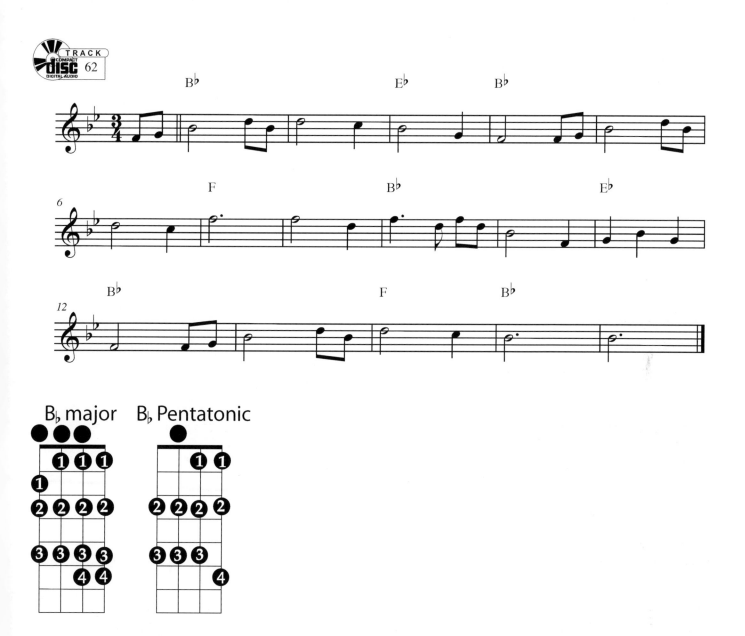

Lesson 61 Harmony in Thirds - B♭

The upper octave should be in easy reach.

Lesson 62: 2/4 Time Signature and the Key of E♭

Many of the tunes so far have been in either 4/4 (Common) time or 2/2 (Cut) time. In 2/4, the four indicates that a quarter note receives one beat. The 2 indicates there are 2 beats per measure. Therefore instead of dealing with quarter and eighth notes as we did in those previously mentioned time signatures, we have eighth and sixteenth notes in 2/4. To count off a tune in 2/4, we simply count 1, 2, 1, 2. Generally 2/4 music will be played faster than 4/4 music. When faced with a measure of eight 16th notes, we can count: *one-ey and ah, two-ey and ah*. They are picked as if they were eighth note in 4/4 with alternating stroke beginning with down.

To read in the key of E♭, first play the first position E♭ scale. Playing the scale preplaces the fingers to play the 3 flats in this key. The author calls the left hand position for this scale *half position,* since the normal first position finger placement is first finger at second fret.

Below is the E♭ major scale. It is followed by the E♭ major arpeggio and the major pentatonic scale. Finally, there are all the possible first position double stops (two note chords.) Remember to start playing the scale from the E♭ note to hear the scale correctly.

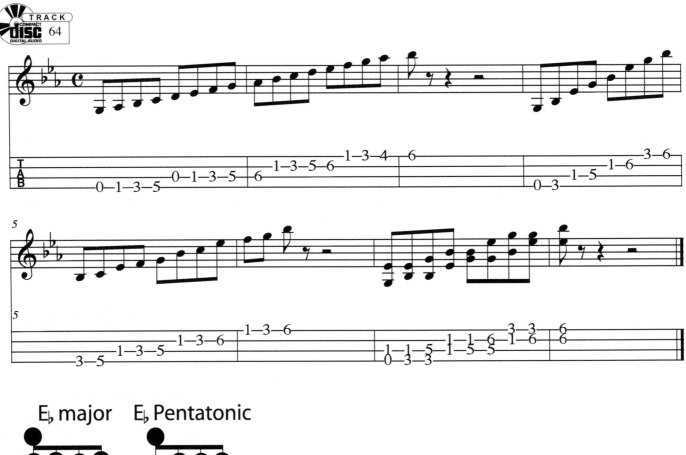

E♭ major   E♭ Pentatonic

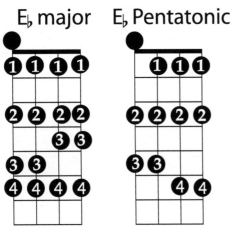

Lesson 63: The E♭ Exercise

Below is the E♭ major reading practice.

Lesson 64: Holmes Hornpipe

Although E♭ might seem to be an unusual key for the mandolin, there are number of hornpipes written in E♭ for the violin/mandolin tuning. The key of E♭ appears often in Scottish violin music collections.

Lesson 65: The Key of A♭

Below is the A♭ major scale. It is followed by the A♭ major arpeggio and the major pentatonic scale. Finally. there are all the possible first position double stops (two note chords.) This is another half position scale.

Lesson 66: A♭ Exercise

Below is some A♭ major practice. Remember the position and proper frets for this key.

Lesson 67: A Flat Hornpipe

Below is a hornpipe written by the author. Be sure to play the A♭ scale in lesson 61 to lock your hand into all the flats needed for this key. Watch for the open (natural) A note in measures 12 and 16.

A♭ major   A♭ Pentatonic

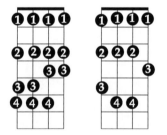

Lesson 68 Harmony in Thirds - A♭

This example should be in easy reach.

Lesson 69: Using Pentatonic Scales to Improvise

Throughout this work pentatonic scale diagrams have appeared next to major scale diagrams. These scales are the quickest path to success for beginning improvisers. *Improvising* is creating original melodies that fit song chord progressions without rehearsal or other preparation.

To understand how to use these scales, we need some music theory. Every key "generates" a set of chords based on the 7 notes in that scale. In C, for example, the chords and their numbers are C (1,) D minor (2,) E minor (3,) D (5,) E minor (6) and F♯diminished (7.) The 2, 3 and 6 chords are minor. In simple country music and folk music around the world, songs are generally written with these chords. The reason is simply that these chords sound good together. Typically, only in jazz, experimental and other "art" musics do we find a songs that venture out of the key for chords.

For beginning improvisors, this is great news. Every note of the major pentatonic scale fits (or sounds good with) all 7 chords generated by a given key. This means that if we know the key of a song, we can use the major pentatonic scale to freely improvise (make up) melodies with no fear of hitting "sour" notes. Now when guitar playing friends ask you to play along as they sing, you will be able. The steps are simple:

1) Ask the key of the song
2) Ask about the chords and determine that they all belong to the key. (They probably will.)
3) Select the appropriate pentatonic scale from the diagrams in this book.
4) Play notes from the scale in any order and rhythm. Be sure to only play notes from the scale.

Memorize scales that are chosen often. If the singer performs regularly in the key of E, memorize that scale. Soloing over chords is a skill that takes practice, but is well worth the time. Listen carefully and note any "bad" notes. Why were they bad? Did you mistakenly play notes not in the scale? There are, of course, other methods to use when soloing, but pentatonic scales are a quick and pleasant way to make great music with others.

Lesson 70: Reading Guitar Manuscripts

The piece on the opposite page was written is the notation style of the classical guitar. Because classical guitarists play with the fingers, it is possible to have 2 moving parts with different length notes in the same measure. When this music is re- arranged for mandolin, a good arranger tries to retain the basic sound of the piece on the new instrument.

Look at measure four of the piece.It contains 2 voices, an upper and lower voice if you will. The upper voice has 4 quarter notes while the lower voice has only a half note during the first half of the measure. To play the measure correctly, strum the double stop on the first beat of the measure and allow the lower note to ring while playing the changing notes on the second string. This "2 ideas at once" playing will be challenging at first, but it is well worth your time.

The next time this approach appears is in measures 9 - 11. In each measure the lower note is allowed to ring three beats (a dotted quarter note) and rests on the fourth beat. In measure 12, the low G and D strings are strummed on beat one and are allowed to ring throughout the four beats of the measure.

In measure 14, the move is somewhat trickier. The B and E notes are allowed to ring for the whole measure while the G# note is picked on beat three. Be careful not to mute the second string when you pick the third. Measures 17-18 are a repeat of measure 9-10.

The phase in measures 19 and 20 may require some awkward fingerings. In measure 19, the third finger frets both the second and third frets. The remaining notes of the measure are picked while the third finger continues to hold the G note. Changing from the 5th to the 4th fret of the A string without stopping the 5th D string may prove ti be a challenge. Perhaps more challenging is measure 20 in which the G is held while notes ascend on the A string including the 5th fret D note.

Measures 21-22 contain one of the most challenging phrases yet with a sustained (tied) A note with a changing note underneath. Needless to say, each of these demanding phrases deserves individual attention and practice.

Lesson 71: Pavan by Milan

This piece was written for vihuela in 1535 by Luis Milan. The *vihuela* (vi-whale-ah) is a small guitar-like instrument with 12 strings. It featues six unison courses (pairs of strings) tuned in fourths similar to the 12 string guitar. The manuscripts from that era were in a tablature form similar to that used today. The vihuela is a plucked instrument (with fingers) and the arranger has adjusted the piece to be played with a pick. This piece was arranged by Gerald Jones who plays mandolin on the accompanying CD.

TRACK
COMPACT
DISC
DIGITAL AUDIO
71

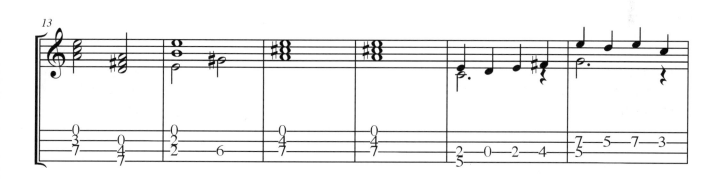

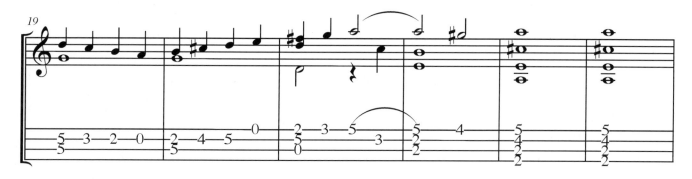

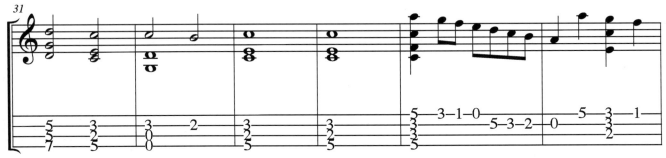

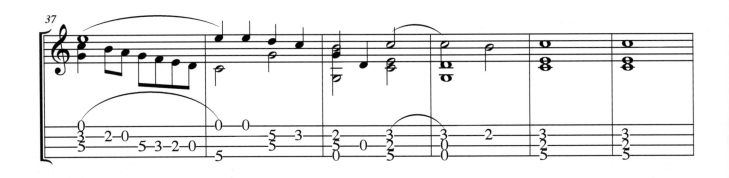

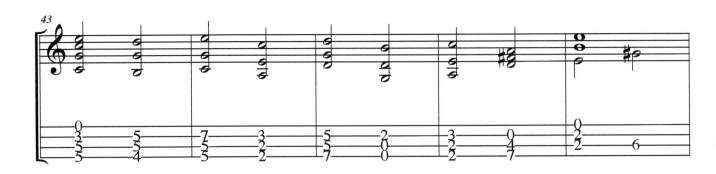

Lesson 72 Harmony in Thirds - G

This example is in easy reach.

Lesson 73: Minor Scales and Chords

To describe minor scales. we must first have an understanding of the major scales we have been playing. The major scale consists of eight notes: Do, Re, Mi, Fa, So, La, Ti and Do. The intervals between the notes are: whole step, whole step, half step, whole step, whole step, whole step, half step. On the mandolin, a half step is one fret and a whole step is two frets. In the example below a G major scale is played up the G string. Of course, we don't play scales in this manner, but the example shows how a major scale is constructed.

There are 3 distinct types of minor scales. The natural minor is the most common. Its formula is: 1, 2, ♭3, 4, 5, 6, 7 and 8. Play any major scale and flatten (lower by 1 fret) the third note of the scale. The example below is a G major scale followed by a G natural minor scale.

This is one way to play the natural minor scale. There is another and perhaps easier way. Every major scale and chord has a relative minor scale and chord. This scale or chord is built on the 6th note (La) of the major scale. For example, we say E minor is the relative minor of G.

Take any major scale. Count as you are playing the scale from the root and stop at the 6th note. Starting with that note, continue to play that major scale. The result is the natural minor scale named for the 6th note of the major scale.The example below is a G major scale followed by an E natural minor scale.

Many musicians memorize the relative minors they use most frequently. Here are several common ones: C: Am, D: Bm, E: C♯m, F: Dm, G: Em and A: F♯m. In written music, since the scales of the major and relative minors are identical, the key signature for the major scale is used for both. For example, a song in E minor is written with one sharp (F♯) in the key signature. For the reader there is no way to know if the song is in E minor or G major unless guitar chords are included.

Lesson 74: Poor Wayfaring Stranger

The key signature of this tune has no sharps or flats. Your experience in this book would lead you to assume the piece is in the key of C. It is however in the relative minor key of A minor.That the piece begins and ends on an A note is a small clue, but there is no way to know for sure unless it is stated somewhere in the music. As you are accustomed to do, play the scale in the key signature before playing the piece to set your fingers to the proper frets.

Lesson 75: Hatikva (The Hope)

Here is the national anthem of Israel. Westerners tend to think of minor keys as sad or dark while in other cultures this is not always the case, Some of the world's most joyous and uplifting songs are written in minor keys. Here is *Hatikva* in the key of E minor, relative of G major.

Lesson 76: Harmony in Thirds - E♭

This example definitely extends beyond practical reach.

Lesson 77: Leontina Mazurka

Here is a two part mazurka in A minor and C major. A muzurka is a European dance in 3/4 time. This tune comes from a 1898 mandolin instruction book entitled *Hamilton's Imperial Mandolin Instructor.*

The piece includes several notes we haven't learned in this book. In measure 11 there is a a C (8th fret, 1st string,) a B (7th fret, 1st string) and an A (5th fret, 1st string.) Finger these as indicated before shifting quickly to continue playing in measure 12. Pay careful attention to the accidentals and listen to the CD for help. Refer to the section on dotted rhythms for extra assistance.

Lesson 78: We Three Kings of Orient Are

Here is a traditional Christmas melody which focuses around E natural minor for the first 16 measures. For the remaining measures, the melody is accompanied by G major chords. The key signature, however, remains the same.

Lesson 79 Harmony in Thirds - D and A

The D example goes well into the hard to reach section of the neck. The A example is more realistic.

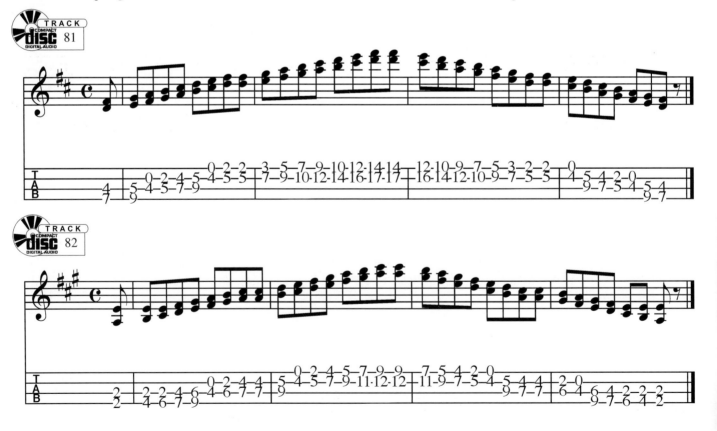

Lesson 80: Major and Minor Pentatonic Scales

Pentatonic scales are five note scales that are commonly used when making up solos to songs. They are useful because they generally fall into easily memorized patterns on the neck and they are a great shortcut for good sounding notes. Major pentatonic scales are presented throughout this book in the keys of C, G, D, A, E, F, B♭, E♭ and A♭. The scale has these intervals: 1, 2, 3, 5 and 6. Below it is shown in the key of G.

The beauty of this scale is that it can be used to freely improvise over most simple chord progressions with no fear of hitting a sour note. This works because the major pentatonic scale doesn't include two notes that can sound bad if they are played at the "wrong" time. These two notes are the 4 and 7 which are great notes but have to be used with care. For beginning improvisers, the pentatonic scale gives us the confidence to try improvising without fear.

Use: Over major chords, when the chords are all derived from the major scale. In other words, the 1, 2 minor, 3 minor, 4, 5 or 6 minor chords. In G these would be G, Am, Bm, C, D and Em. In practice, this means the concept works for 100's of songs since songs are very often written to include only these chords. Why? These chords sound good together.

Sound: The sound of this scale can be characterized as "bright," "happy" or a major country music sound. The lead themes to The Temptation's "My Girl," Pure Prairie League's "Amie" and Merle Haggard's "Rambling Fever" are examples major pentatonic scales.

The minor pentatonic scale has these intervals: 1. ♭3, 4, 5 and ♭7. Below it is shown in G.

Use: 1) Over minor chords or progressions. 2) Over major chords or progressions when a bluesy or rock sound is desired.

Sound: The sound of the scale can be characterized as "dark," "sad" (over minor chords) or "bluesy" or "rock" (over major chords.)

The surprising feature of these two scales is that the major and relative minor pentatonic scales are identical! In the key of C, the major pentatonic scale is C (1,) D (2,) E (3,) G (5) and A (6.) In A minor, the minor pentatonic scale is A (1,) C (♭3,) D(4,) E (5) and G (♭7.) Therefore, the same set of 5 notes are both the major and minor pentatonic of C and A minor. The example below shows these two scales played from their respective roots.

Lesson 81: Sakura (Cherry Blossom)

Here is a traditional Japanese melody which is pentatonic (A, B, C, E and F) but is not clearly major or minor. Pentatonic scales come in many varieties throughout the musical world.

Lesson 82 Harmony in Thirds - E

This example also extends beyond practical reach.

Lesson 83: Scale Patterns for Practice

   Below is an ascending and descending G major scale followed by several scale patterns. These patterns should be played repeatedly until they are familiar. The next step is to apply them to each major scale presented in this work. By playing the patterns in each key, you will becme familiar with the keys and develop increased left hand/right hand coordination.

Conclusion

Congratulations! By completing this volume you are well prepared to be a successful mandolin player. Your next step is to determine what type of mandolin music attracts you. You may be able to find a teacher with the same interests or a book that specializes in your favorite style. Mel Bay Publications has an extensive library of mandolin books including a number I have written at melbay.com.

Find a mandolin playing friend and use the duets in this volume to begin making music with others. Solitary music study is rewarding but only in a social music setting will your new mandolin playing hobby reach its full potential. Congratulations again for choosing the mandolin and for dedicating yourself to making good music. Your musical journey has just begun!

Photo by Gerald Jones.

About the Author

Since 1985, Joe Carr has been a music instructor specializing in Bluegrass, Western Swing and Irish music in the Commercial Music program at South Plains College in Levelland, Texas. He is a director for Camp Bluegrass, a summer residential Music camp in its 25th year (2011.)

In 1977, Joe joined the internationally known *Country Gazette* bluegrass band with banjo player Alan Munde and bluegrass legend Roland White. Joe appeared on three group albums, a solo album and numerous other recorded projects during his seven-year tenure with the band. In the 1990s, Carr and Munde formed a duo that toured extensively throughout the U.S., Canada and England and recorded two albums for Flying Fish/Rounder Records.

Joe has developed and appeared in over thirty instructional music videos for Mel Bay Publications and Texas Music & Video. He has written many instructional book/CD combinations for Mel Bay and has a growing number of DVDs available. Included are diverse titles such as *Western Swing Fiddle* MB20289BCD, *Mandolin Gospel Tunes* MB20554BCD and *School of Country Guitar* MB21645BCD.

Joe is a regular columnist for *Flatpicking Guitar Magazine* and *Mandolin Magazine*. He is the editor for Mel Bay's webzine Mandolin Sessions.
melbay.com/mandolinsessions

In 1996, the Texas Tech University Press published *Prairie Nights to Neon Lights: The Story of Country Music in West Texas* by Carr and Munde. Joe can be seen and heard at acousticmusician.com/JoeCarr.html